Altered Reflections that Hinder Success

The War In The Mirror II

Dr. Janice Crenshaw

ISBN 979-8-89619-360-9

Table of Contents

The War in The Mirror

When you look in the mirror, what do you see? The immediate image of what is a physical reality comes into view. The portrait of fact is sometimes appealing and sometimes not, especially the first thing in the morning after awakening from a long night's sleep. Now for some of us ladies, this may be more startling for those who refuse to sleep without the mask of makeup. However, there is an immediate assessment of how we see ourselves in that moment. There is an old saying that goes, "What you see, is what you get." Is this true? What you already have could be more than what you see. This very fact ignites a physical and emotional war from within that could potentially create internal conflict. This conflict goes far beyond what one sees when they look in the mirror. One's visual view of self, whether we want to admit it or not, is influenced by many other variables in this journey called *life*. The objective of this book is to evaluate those variables and determine strategies that will serve as an antidote to many of the obstacles that cause us to forfeit our destiny.

The challenge begins with having the ability to separate external influences and issues of others from one's own internal struggles. We will examine how to identify external issues that has nothing to do with you, from internal issues that plague one's view of self-worth. Let's consider Moses who forfeited his opportunity to walk into the promise land because he internalized the external issues that he was experiencing with the Children of Israel, who were rebellious and constantly murmuring and complaining. Instead of him speaking to the rock, as the Lord had instructed him to do... he smote the rock. What in your life have you internalized that is not your issue? Taking ownership of what does not belong to you causes you to internalize warfare that takes away valuable time and energy that could be used to pursue your dreams in life.

Let's consider the analogy of a broken mirror. One cannot see the reality of what really is, when you look at yourself through a broken mirror. There are cracks, and shattered pieces of the mirror that alter the true reflection of the reality. To continue to try and get a clear view, through a broken mirror, is a waste of time and will only distort what you are striving to visualize. So, it is with life. Warfare begins with broken pieces and shattered dreams that have been influenced by what we have chosen to see about ourselves. Emotional wars have occurred in everyone's life at some time or another. A war that was not always created by you, but sometimes we invite unnecessary warfare into our place of passion by becoming intimate with external issues of others. Have you ever been in a relationship or friendship with someone and suddenly it goes sour for some unknown reason, and you ask yourself, "What did I do?" We sometimes spend sleepless nights trying to understand the immediate shift in one's behavior. Well, this book will help you to understand that many times it is not you, at all. The enemy of your destiny has orchestrated a plan to get your focus off track by consuming your emotional energy on something you cannot control to detour you away from your destiny.

You will never be able to control another person's behavior, you can only control your own.

Stop right now and quote the 'serenity prayer' that we have heard so many times before. Allow this prayer to be a daily reminder to release whatever is clouding your vision to visualize beyond what you see about yourself.

O God and Heavenly Father, Grant to us the serenity of mind to accept that which cannot be changed; courage to change that which can be changed, and wisdom to know the one from the other, through Jesus Christ our Lord, Amen.

In this book, we will explore three aspects of overcoming the War in the Mirror.

What altered reflections are you seeing about yourself.

Why are these reflections so real, but yet so inaccurate?

How to overcome these altered reflections to walk into your divine destiny.

There is one requirement that is necessary to be able to experience the freedom you so long for in your spiritual and emotional being......*you must be honest.* Make a conscious decision to open your mind and spirit to personally evaluate your mirrors of life and determine if *"What you see, is what you get"* or is *"What you already have is more than what you see".* Let's begin the journey to first evaluate what is fact and what is fiction.

CHAPTER 1

Is it Fact or Fiction?

I want to begin this chapter with a very practical approach to something most of us do every day, and that is watch TV, or maybe other social media entertainment sites. Now some may be a little more over the top with watching television than others, but at some time or another most of us have engaged in watching a very inspiring movie, or the latest movie that has been released. Just for reference, consider the TV series Greenleaf on the OWN network. The story line of Greenleaf depicts the so-called daily lifestyle of church folk, from the pulpit to the door, from the choir stand to the church cafeteria, and from the church office to the bedroom at home. However, as symbolic as this TV series may be to real life, the actual story is fiction for those who are playing the roles. Now I can hear some of you saying right now....... "Not really", because this kind of stuff is happening every day in the church. How sad that may be true. But herein lies the challenge of being able to draw the line between what is fact and what is fiction in the immediate assessment of any situation. It takes a strong Will to not internalize what we see even in movies. Think for a moment, what movie have you seen that took you to a place maybe you did, or did not want to go? This is not intentional, it just validates the power that what we visualize can have on how we think, respond, and behave. Some have left the movie theater happy, mad, sad, and some ready to fight depending on the story line. However, much of what we saw was all fiction, unless it was based on a true story. Although the story line may be symbolic to life in general, it is not all fact in every aspect of what you saw. And even for those movies that are based on a true story, it is fiction for the characters who are playing the part of another person's actual life experiences. This is where the real test begins. Now think about this... how many times have you internalized what you saw in a movie, went home, looked in the mirror and saw reflections of yourself based on what you just saw. Now is this reflection real or is it altered? Only you can answer that question. It reminds me of the scripture in **Hebrews 4:12** (KJV)- *"For the Word of God is quick, and powerful, and sharper than any two-edged sword, piercing even to the dividing asunder of soul and spirit, and of the joints and mar-*

row, and is a discerner of the thoughts and intents of the heart."

This is how sensitive the challenge is to determine what is fact or fiction, when we have allowed external issues into our personal space of passion. Only the truth of God's Word concerning who the heavenly Father has called you to be can decode false reflections of who you really are. *"For I know the thoughts that I think toward you, saith the* LORD, *thoughts of peace, and not of evil, to give you an expected end."*- **Jeremiah 29:11 (KJV)**

I personally recall seeing the movie Hotel Rwanda. This movie was based on a true story of a real holocaust in which the Hutu tribe set out to kill all the Tutsis for revenge for the killing of the Hutu king. This movie impacted me in so many ways because I internalized many of the coded messages in the movie. These coded messages caused me to see myself in a different light. However, not distorted, but this movie gave me a clearer picture of who I really was. I suggest you watch this movie and research the documentary for historical details of fact. It will change your life. When I looked in the mirror, I saw fact, and no longer fiction, that had for so long been presented as fact. I did not internalize the killings. I did not internalize the spirit of hate in this movie. I paid attention to the hidden codes. These hidden factual codes changed the spiritual DNA of my thoughts and launched my passion to succeed to another level. Herein lies your determined Will to choose what you do with reflections that may appear to be all negative. Learn how to turn man's facts about you into fiction. Instead of allowing others to turn fiction into your fact.

Stop owning another man's story line that is not your own.

There are hidden codes everywhere in this journey of life on your way to your divine destiny. What the enemy wants to do is to get you caught up with immediate emotional responses to what you see in your own personal mirror of life verses learning how to decode the hidden facts that are far beyond what you see. Remember, *what you already have may be more than what you see.* This next chapter will reveal how to begin the journey to be able to decode hidden facts about you that have been seen by others as just a fictional story line. Let's go!!

CHAPTER 2

Internal Vs External Issues

The journey to decode fiction that has been presented as fact starts with your ability to reject ownership of what does not belong to you. Success can be buried and distorted by allowing what never was....to become the compass for the decisions you make, the company you keep and places you go.

It is time to give Fiction an eviction notice today!

Let's begin by exploring three principles: Right People, Right Place and Right Approach. These principles will help guide your journey to your divine place of purpose, and help you discern between internal issues that are areas in your life you should evaluate and allow the Holy Spirt to help you overcome, and external issues that are influenced by relationships, our environment, and how we see ourselves that many times have nothing to do with your true purpose in life.

Right People is a link to divine destiny

Life is an all-inclusive journey of meeting different people who come from a diversity of backgrounds. Some individuals you are grateful your paths crossed and some you wish you had never set eyes on them. Sadly, some of these encounters cannot be avoided because our lives are full of day-to-day responsibilities and obligations that put us in the position to have to deal with individuals occasionally in ways we would prefer not to. For an example, have you ever simply dreaded going to work because you knew you had to deal with a toxic work environment? However, you must work. This is a great example of external issues that can impact your internal emotions if you are not careful. It becomes a daily frustrating challenge to be able to shift your focus on your assignment and not allow what you cannot control to become your burden.

Having been in health care for decades and experiencing a diversity of cultural settings in the workplace, has afforded me many pleasant moments of professional growth with a variety of opportunities. However, there were some cultural experiences that were beyond my comprehension of what I would call a safe and trusting work environment. In some cases, a total embarrassment to the definition of professionalism. Herein was my daily challenge....to not *internalize* the toxicity of an *external* work environment that I could not control and focus on seeing my job as an assignment with a specific purpose.   One's ability to be successful in their assignment has nothing to do with the questionable character of those of whom are responsible for creating an unhealthy work environment for others. Not being able to separate this external issue from your internal purpose will only distort your personal perception of your professional potential.

Never see yourself through the lens of another man's inappropriate behavior. It is an external issue that is trying to invade your purpose...reject it and keep it moving!!

I want to shift the paradigm of thought here to deal with this from a relationship perspective. Have you ever encountered meeting the wrong person that turned out to be the right person to get you to the right place in life? Some relationships are used by God as a catalyst to propel you to the next level. These are external connections that should never be integrated into your internal circle of relationships. But should be respected only for the purpose that God has ordained and nothing more!

Let's consider Esther in the Bible who was chosen to be Queen after Vashti refused to come into the presence of the King.

Esther 1:10-12 King James Version (KJV) *[10] On the seventh day, when the heart of the king was merry with wine, he commanded Mehuman, Biztha, Harbona, Bigtha, and Abagtha, Zethar, and Carcas, the seven chamberlains that served in the presence of Ahasuerus the king, [11] To bring Vashti the queen before the king with the crown royal, to shew the people and the princes her beauty: for she was fair to look on. [12] But the queen Vashti refused to come at the king's commandment by his chamberlains: therefore, was the king very wroth, and his anger burned in him.*

Because Queen Vashti refused to respond to the commandment of the King, he sent out a decree in search for another Queen. Esther was chosen out of all the maidens the King rejected. Esther not only had beauty, but she had favor. The bad decision of one person, Queen Vashti, opened the door for Esther to be Queen. The wrong person, with wrong choices, might be the right person for your next miracle. If God allowed it, then He will turn a bad encounter, that is not directly connected to you, into a positive outcome for your benefit.

"Acknowledge God in all your ways, and He will direct your path" - **Proverbs 3:6**.

To acknowledge God in all your ways will help you to better understand that those of whom you feel are right for you, may just be wrong for you. And the person you feel is wrong may just be the right person who could be the link to your success. The ability to understand this spiritual paradigm will enable you to evaluate the "Why?" behind every personal encounter and relationship that God allows. However, never accept what God has rejected. You will only open the door to an unnecessary emotional war that will distort the reality of your true purpose.

Right Place positions you for favor

Esther's journey got her to the right place to fulfill her purpose. But it took the behavior of Queen Vashti who was clearly seen as the wrong person in the eyes of the King. However, Queen Vashti was the right person to get Esther to the right place.

Esther 4:14 King James Version (KJV) *[14] For if thou altogether holdest thy peace at this time, then shall there enlargement and deliverance arise to the Jews from another place; but thou and thy father's house shall be destroyed: and who knoweth whether thou art come to the kingdom for such a time as this?*

The Right Place is always masked by challenges and delays. Esther was challenged with deciding whether she should go in unto the King unannounced to save the lives of God's people. The benefits of being in the right place can only be activated by using the right approach. Esther's approach to fast and pray before going in before the King granted her access that could not be denied. If the approach you are using is not working, even though you know you are in the right place, you should consult the Lord.

Esther 4:16 (KJV) *[16] Go, gather together all the Jews that are present in Shushan, and fast ye for me, and neither eat nor drink three days, night or day: I also and my maidens will fast likewise; and so will I go in unto the king, which is not according to the law: and if I perish, I perish.*

When the disciples had toiled all night long and had not caught any fish, Jesus instructed them to cast their nets on the right side of the ship. If what you are doing is not working, maybe God is leading you in a new direction. However, we must be mindful to have faith in God. Some things are not going to happen overnight. You must trust God and know that He will do just what He said. The disciples obeyed the instructions of Jesus and caught a multitude of fish, so much so that their nets began to break **(St. John 21:6)**. The key is obedience to the direction of the Lord that should never be influenced by your emotions.

My husband, Bishop John Crenshaw and I pastored for almost 40 years collectively in two different states. We began our journey with only seven members. We were very young at the time. I was in my late 20's and my husband in his mid-30's. It was not popular at that time for husband and wife to pastor as a team as some call it today, Co-Pastors. We endured the challenges of many attempts to mock what God had favored us to obtain by those who looked upon us with an eye of criticism, and how could we pull this off and survive. We quickly learned that if God has called the husband, He has also called the wife as his help meet. And if they are not both in it together, it will quickly be discerned, and a door is quickly opened to the enemy. There were many shifting seasons in our ministry for over thirty years. Some came and went. But by the Grace of God, we survived the storms. This journey taught us many things and favored us the Wisdom to know when to take another turn. Turns that were purposed to catch the enemy off guard. This can only be accomplished through a life of prayer and being sensitive to the voice of God. Some have asked "What did that first day in pastoring look like?" Well, it looked like the favor of God for a young couple in the 1980's, to buy a church with just seven people. It felt right and good. However, the fact of being responsible for the souls of people quickly became a heartfelt reality from that day forward. This is a serious matter. We knew we had to build the ministry around the importance of prayer. Prayer helped us to realize that it does not take a lot of people supporting you to propel you into your divine purpose. We saw the ministry grow, with the mission to impact the community that granted us favor with many community leaders. However, beyond Day #1, our goal was to grow with influence that would result in winning Souls to Jesus Christ.

If your influence is not larger than your immediate audience, you just have a number

We committed to get to know some of the Pastors in the city as the Lord would direct us to. We also did a historical research of the city, when and how it was founded. What was the background of the first persons who settled in the area? This helped us to understand the underlying warfare that we would have to contend with. A study of the demographics helped us to better understand how the diversity of the population would impact church growth. With a population in the 1990's of 70% Caucasian and 22% Black, and the remaining percentage of other ethnic backgrounds, there were over 200 black churches and 140 Caucasian churches in this city. Based on the population of both the county and the city, statistically you can only have approximately 900 members per church. However, many do not go to church and racial diversity is another factor to consider, because most people usually choose to attend a church where most of the people look like them. Taking into consideration all these barriers and variables......the average black church in this area with at least 200 to 300 members is statistically successful because the bodies are simply not in the geographical area. This level of research will help any leader who may be feeling unsuccessful because of the number of people attending their church to understand how to separate external factors that may be influencing their internal purpose. The mission should always be to focus on your assignment, understand the "why" behind the warfare, pray, seek God for a strategic plan, and you will be successful. Your assignment might be different from what is assumed to be identified as successful ministry. It will prevent one from falling prey to the spirit of competition, division and warfare against the brethren who seem to appear more successful. There were many other research related findings about the founding of the city that I will not specifically share in this book, which helped to explain the economic and spiritual culture of the area. Herein, again prayer is the key. For those who desire to research this further, I encourage you to take time to study your geographical territory and ask God for spiritual guidance. Territorial warfare is real and is present in every city. It can impact how you see yourself as being effective in ministry. Learning how to identify external issues is crucial to keeping you focused on what you have been called to do. What you are desiring to accomplish in life is dependent upon how you respond to these external issues that have nothing to do with you and your God given assignment.

I want to stop right here and pray for every city across this globe and declare that it is a place of blessings, where the Word is rich, Churches and Pastors are unified and spirit of witchcraft, division and manipulation is defeated, in Jesus Name.

Right approach grants access to your next miracle

All of what has been discussed, thus far, is how external issues can create internal storms that you can spend years trying to overcome. When I look back over almost 40 years of pastoring, there were many challenges, but overall, it was a wonderful journey. Take time to understand exactly what you are dealing with. I have learned to live by this quote to keep spiritual balance regarding external variables that I cannot control.

It's not that serious, keep it moving
Success is defined within the walls of your assignment, not within the walls of another man's accomplishments.

This is the spiritual antidote for the spirit of competition, division and political manipulation that can so easily creep in and create unnecessary additional warfare. Always remember that *people are not your enemy.*

Ephesians 6:12 (KJV) *[12] For we wrestle not against flesh and blood, but against principalities, against powers, against the rulers of the darkness of this world, against spiritual wickedness in high places.*

When Believers function as the Ecclesia as Jesus so ordained it to be (the called-out ones to govern, i.e. schools, finances, etc.), you will not be liked by everyone, but your life will speak for itself and respect will be granted.

Live to be respected, not liked

"Woe unto you when all men speak well of you."- **(St. Luke 6:26)**

Every level in life that the Lord allows you to experience must include a strategic approach to accomplish your assignment. Transitioning from one city to another to establish ministry, for us, required another level of strategic thinking to do Kingdom work because of the very diverse culture.... economically, intellectually, and spiritually.

Thinking outside the box is traditional, getting rid of the box and then start thinking is Kingdom

However, every territory carries its own set of spiritual battles. I was favored to be hired by the state to direct the implementation of a Quality department for one of their divisions. During my time with the organization, I could not understand why so many of the black employees seemed to be afraid to be seen talking to one another. There was a sense of fear and intimidation that radiated throughout the facility with a subtle message to just stay in your place. This concerned me, so I decided to do some research, which revealed that the downtown location of the place of employment was the same place where the Lawyers offices were located for the sale of slaves. Well that answered my concern. That spirit was still deeply rooted in this territory, and only the Power of God could break it. It was evident that many had embraced external forces that were impacting their internal peace and freedom.

As Believers, we must know that God has not called us to every assignment in the earth. Some things are not for you to deal with and can become a distraction to doing what you were called to do.

When the mountain won't move...Leave it

And that is exactly what the Lord afforded to happen. Do not waste any time trying to fix what God has rejected on your behalf. He will redeem all things unto himself in His timing. He has something greater in view.

Deuteronomy 2:1-3 (KJV) *[1] Then we turned and took our journey into the wilderness by the way of the Red sea, as the Lord spake unto me: and we compassed mount Seir many days. [2] And the Lord spake unto me, saying, [3] Ye have compassed this mountain long enough: turn you northward.*

As I close this chapter, I admonish you to reflect upon the principles that have been given and incorporate them into your strategic goal setting for your life. Many examples I have shared were relative to Ministry leaders and Pastors. However, these principles can be applied to any person who is striving to find their way through life's challenges, trying to overcome stereotypical labels that may result in you not seeing yourself as God sees you. A person can be one step away from their next breakthrough and mess it up with the wrong approach, because of the many cultural pressures. Look closely at the life of Moses, a type of Christ, who was called to lead the Children of Israel out of the land of Egypt, just as Jesus came to bring us out of a life of sin (a type of Egypt). Those of us who have read our Bibles, know that the Children of Israel were rebellious and a stiff neck people who were not happy with the leadership of Moses.

"And the LORD said unto Moses, I have seen this people, and, behold, it is a stiff neck people:"- **Exodus 32:9 (KJV)**

"Then they said to Moses, "Because there were no graves in Egypt, have you taken us away to die in the wilderness? Why have you so dealt with us, to bring us up out of Egypt?"- **Exodus 14:11 (NKJV)**

The Lord told Moses to speak to the rock, but instead he smote the rock and missed his opportunity to go into the promised land. He internalized external issues of a rebellious people that caused him to miss his blessing. Don't allow external issues to become your internal storm and miss what God has for you. If folk want to hate you, let them hate by themselves. If folk want to be indifferent- let them be indifferent by themselves. *"Keep it moving"*. You have much work to do for the Kingdom.

Let's pray this prayer. Father in the name of Jesus, I reject every external influence that has come to distort my kingdom view of who I am called to be and what I am called to do. I will not accept another fictious storyline that is built on deeply rooted spirits of darkness. It has nothing to do with me. These are external issues that I refuse to embrace. I reject them in the name of Jesus. I accept the fact that I am redeemed by the Blood of Jesus, and I am more than a Conqueror through Jesus Christ who loves me. No evil shall befall me or come nigh my dwelling. Amen.

In this next chapter we will explore how internal issues can impact your emotional and spiritual health and hinder healthy Kingdom relationships.

Chapter 3
Mirrors of the Midnight

Consider this question. "Who did you sleep with last night?" I'm sure immediately your mind went back to the last intimate moment with your spouse or an intimate relationship of the past. But I want to provoke spiritual thought. "What spirit did you sleep with last night?' Was it jealousy, envy, bitterness, unforgiveness, hatred, or strife? Maybe you are someone who just can't seem to get over the fact that your father or some other relative molested you when you were a child, or your spouse left you for someone else and the hurt has grown into bitterness and even hatred. Maybe a professing Christian you trusted touched you in an ungodly way when you were a child and you have not shared it with anyone. Or maybe you have experienced so called church hurt by those who say they are believers. The memory of these experiences is readily prevalent in your mind, and you refuse to forgive. Jesus declared in the Word that you must forgive.

"Let not the sun go down on your wrath"- **Ephesians 4:26**

Don't allow yourself to become intimate with unclean spirits and give them permission to take up residence within you. Unclean spirits are looking for a place of rest and they find rest in the lives of people.

"When an unclean spirit is gone out of a man, he walketh through dry places, seeking rest." – **St. Luke 11:14**

Man was created to glorify God. Therefore, when an unclean spirit enters the life of an individual, he is not at peace with God to whom he was created to worship. He is usually very unhappy and miserable. Unclean spirits, such as unforgiveness and bitterness become a part of an individual's spiritual makeup, and whatever they attempt to accomplish will be affected.

"Know ye not that your body is the temple of the Holy Ghost."- **I Corinthians 6:19**

I'm reminded of a sister in the Lord who had a relative who consistently sexually abused her when she was a child. When she told her mother, she did not want to believe this because the relative was her brother. This Spirit-filled Believer had held on to this for years, without sharing it with anyone.

She came to me one day and shared that she was having difficulty being intimate with her husband. She shared the years of sexual abuse by her uncle when she was a child. I asked her, had she ever told her uncle that she had forgiven him. She said, "No". I asked her, "Why not?" She stated that he had been in prison for years and she has not seen him. It was evident that she had not forgiven her uncle. I encouraged her to sit down and write her uncle a letter in prison, tell him that she forgives him for what he had done to her, and that she was praying for his salvation. She wrote the letter and was set free. She was no longer bound spending restless nights being intimate with the spirit of unforgiveness.

Life experiences that have negatively touched the most intimate areas of one's life can have a lasting effect, resulting in feelings of defeat, despair, and frustration. One can find themselves spending sleepless nights trying to rid themselves of the hurt and pain of relationships or experiences that have devastated their life. You go to bed and awaken with unhealthy feelings of anger and revenge. Everyday seems to be repetitive rehearsal of things in the past.

You will never be able to move on in life without forgiveness because the other person you refuse to forgive is holding you hostage. Decide today to be free. If you do not forgive, your heavenly Father will not forgive you.

Judges 2:17 (KJV) *17 "And yet they would not hearken unto their judges, but they went a whoring after other gods, and bowed themselves unto them: they turned quickly out of the way which their fathers walked in, obeying the commandments of the Lord; but they did not so."*

Judges 2:17 speaks of Israel whoring after other Gods. The Lord was not speaking in the natural sense, but spiritually. Israel had become intimate with idol gods. It is easy to become intimate with bitterness, unforgiveness, hatred and strife as a result of devastating situations in one's life, spending countless hours ministering to their past hurts and pain instead of ministering unto God, who can deliver.

Don't put yourself in a position to birth your own enemy who will fight against you in your own house

Think about Abraham and Sarah whom the Lord promised them a son in their old age. Sarah thought this was so ridiculous that she laughed at this possibility. As a result, she made a conscious decision to help God out and requested that Abraham go into Hagar to have a child. When Ismael was born, Sarah became bitter with Hagar and Ishmael, and wanted Abraham to send them both away. What Sarah failed to realize is that she made a decision that birthed her own enemy who fought against her in her own house. Her lack of faith led her to become so bitter that she felt that giving her husband to another woman was the answer to birthing her heart's desire. For whatsoever is not of faith is sin (**Romans 14:23**), which can cause one to make decisions that will bring unnecessary pain.

I am sure as you are reflecting upon this story, you can recall times when you have made wrong decisions that have impacted your life in a negative way. We all have. But thank God for His Grace. He will take the worse situation and turn it for our good.

Romans 8:28 (KJV) *28 "And we know that all things work together for good to them that love God, to them who are the called according to his purpose."*

He will take what most would see as a disgrace and cause His Grace to turn it into a blessing. Ask

Joseph who was about to put Mary, the mother of Jesus, away because she was pregnant but had never been with a man. God has a plan for our lives even when we make bad decisions. Stop being intimate with the bad decisions you have made. Let it go! Allow God to take a mess and give you a message to deliver others. Allow the Lord to turn your midnight pain into morning miracles.

Psalms 30:5, **(KJV)** *"For his anger endureth but a moment; in his favour is life: weeping may endure for a night, but joy cometh in the morning."*

In this next chapter, we will discuss how important it is to live out destiny by conceiving in your heart God's plan for your life, and the challenges we face striving to submit to His perfect Will.

CHAPTER 4

Mirrors of Conception "Oh no I'm having twins!"

For women who have experienced having twins, I'm sure you can probably remember how you felt when the doctor informed you that you were pregnant, with not just one baby, but two. I can imagine you felt many things.....from happiness to despair, especially if you were not emotionally prepared for the news. Something happened in the process of reproduction that produced the fertilization of two eggs. In **St. Luke 8:11**, *Jesus declared that the seed is the Word of God. Some seeds fell by the wayside, some fell upon rocks, and some fell on thorns, but the seeds that fell on good ground are they, which is an honest and good heart, having heard the Word, kept it and brought forth fruit.* Many Believers are trying to lead a double life. They want to obey God, but they lack discipline and responsibility. James said a "double minded man is unstable in all his ways" (**St. James 1:8**). There is a constant war within the mind that breeds instability in every area of life.

Consider the story of Esau and Jacob in the Twenty-Fifth Chapter of Genesis. Rebecca inquired of the Lord as to why Esau and Jacob struggled within her womb. The Lord answered Rebecca by saying that she had two nations in her womb and two manners of people. Esau and Jacob were totally different in character.

Genesis 25:24-34 (KJV) [24] *"And when her days to be delivered were fulfilled, behold, there were twins in her womb."* [25] *"And the first came out red, all over like an hairy garment; and they called his name Esau."* [26] *"And after that came his brother out, and his hand took hold on Esau's heel; and his name was called Jacob":*

I'm sure those nine months for Rebecca were quite uncomfortable. Not only was she carrying two children, but the twins she carried were very active and at war with one another. Imagine nine months of this kind of activity in the womb. It is very difficult to rest and it's extremely uncomfortable.

Are there things warring within your spirit that have been conceived through devastating experiences in your life? Or are you trying to live out your dreams through another man's success because you feel less worthy. Although you've heard the Word and conceived the Word in your heart, somewhere in the process of your spiritual growth, you missed God and allowed the seed of failure to grow. You awakened one morning and realized... "Oh no, I am having twins." There is something else going on in your spirit that is not in alignment with the Word you received from the Lord.

In **Genesis 25:23**, God spoke a Word into Rebecca's womb that Esau would serve Jacob. Esau was the elder son, and Jacob was the younger. It was not custom for the elder son to serve the younger. I believe this Word from God created a war between the two brothers, even before they were born.

Genesis 25:23 (KJV) *"And the Lord said unto her, Two nations are in thy womb, and two manner of people shall be separated from thy bowels; and the one people shall be stronger than the other people; and the elder shall serve the younger."*

God's Word will create an unrest within you when there are seeds that have been released in your spirit that do not connect with your divine destiny. You will not be able to rest. Allow the Word of God to conceive on good ground and immediately begin to nourish it in your heart with obedience and submission to His Will for your life. Begin to see yourself as God sees you, versus striving to measure up to the perception of how others see you. What the Lord has purposed for you to bring forth in this earth is unique. Unlike any other. Sometimes we create unnecessary warfare because although we desire to do the Will of God, we are also trying to measure up to the expectations of others to validate our success......two natures fighting one against the other, going nowhere fast.

Let's talk about Ananias and Sapphira in the Fifth Chapter of Acts. They made a covenant decision together to lie to the Holy Ghost. Sapphira did not know that Ananias had fell dead when she came in and told the same lie that her husband had told. She too fell dead.

Acts 5:3 (KJV), *"But Peter said, Ananias, why hath Satan filled thine heart to lie to the Holy Ghost, and to keep back part of the price of the land?"*

Notice Peter said, "filled thine heart". This lie had been conceived in the heart of both Ananias and Sapphira and they made a soulish decision to lie to God. Man is a spirit, who lives in a body and possesses a soul. The soul is your mind and emotions. Ananias and Sapphira agreed in their minds (soul) to keep back part of the possession, this lie was conceived in their hearts which caused them to sin in the flesh.

The Lord has declared that all souls are mine. It belongs to God. No one has the right to possess your soul or control your mind. Even though God made Ananias and Sapphira one flesh as husband and wife, He did not say they were one Soul. That part of you belongs to God and Him alone. When anyone attempts to covenant with you to disobey the Word or Will of God, someone must take a stand and obey the Truth. Like Job, who was able to say to his wife, that *she talked like a foolish woman* when she told him to curse God and die. He refused to make a covenant decision with his wife that was totally against the Will of God.

Although God has given us the choice to make right decisions, based on His Word and His Will for our lives, we are not to take this out of spiritual context and not respect the opinions of our spouses and find ourselves walking outside God's plan for our lives, because one may feel they are always right. Paul explained in **I Corinthians 7:3-5** that the husband and the wife should render due benevolence one to another. The woman hath not power over her own body, but the husband; and likewise, also the husband hath not power over his body, but the wife. Notice once again, the scripture did not say that he woman or the man had power over the Soul. We all need the mind of Christ.

Philippians 2:5 (KJV) *"Let this mind be in you, which was also in Christ Jesus."*

As we conclude this chapter think back over the journey of your life, are you struggling with fulfilling the call of God, because maybe you have made covenant with that which was not God's Will for you? Are you trying to birth destiny through the eyes of another man's accomplishment and as result there is a constant warfare from within? ..... two natures that conflict with one another. I encourage you to take a moment and right down your goals and ask yourself ...are these goals based on what God has confirmed is His Will for your life, or are they goals that have been birthed through pain and disappointment, lack of confidence in who God has called you to be, or low self-esteem?   As a result, you spend more time being who you are not, versus who you already are, in God's plan for your life.

Decide today to rise above the war from within, stand in the mirror and declare that you are wonderfully made by the hand of God and your uniqueness cannot be duplicated. Pray to remain humble in all you do and remember that Greater is

He that is in you than he that is in the world. In this next chapter we will discuss how important it is to get rid of every seed that is not connected to the God's plan for your life to avoid miscarriage of your divine destiny.

CHAPTER 5

The Mirror of Release (miscarriage vs. abortion)

A *miscarriage* is defined by Webster as the failure to carry out what was intended, or the birth of a baby before it has developed enough to live. Let's look at this same definition and relate it to the destiny that has been assigned to your life. Satan wants you to miscarriage your dreams, your vision, and your goals before they have been fully developed. He does this by attacking the most sensitive areas of your life (i.e. your family, your finances, friends who walk away, etc.), to keep you from carrying out what has been conceived in your heart through the Word of God. When a woman is threatening a miscarriage, she must be very cautious and careful about her levels of activity, her diet, and the amount of rest she gets. There are times we can become so busy doing none of what God has called us to do that we become exhausted and eventually loose vision that was given to us by God. And if we do not watch our spiritual diet, we will begin to feast on that which is not good for overall success.

An *abortion* may be defined as the spontaneous or induced explosion of the products of conception before the fetus is legally viable. The word abortion is commonly used in the context of a willful desire of a woman to get rid of a child before it is born. The decision to abort a child could be based on several reasons, whether it be that the child has some type of abnormality, or the mother simply doesn't want the lifelong responsibility of taking care of a child. *Allow me to clarify. I do not condone abortion as a luxury, just because the mother does not want to have the child.* Let's consider this spiritually. Many times, in our lives, we can allow seeds of un-forgiveness, bitterness, hatred, envy, strife and other works of the flesh to harbor so long in our hearts until it causes one to begin to make bad decisions and that's totally against God's Will.

Galatians 5:19-21 (KJV) [19] *"Now the works of the flesh are manifest, which are these; Adultery, fornication, uncleanness, lasciviousness,* [20] *Idolatry, witchcraft, hatred, variance, emulations, wrath, strife, seditions, heresies,* [21] *Envyings, murders, drunkenness, revellings, and such like: of the which I tell you before, as I have also told you in time past, that they which do such things shall not inherit the kingdom of God."*

When we identify that these works of the flesh are hindering our Will to obey God, we need to willfully go before Him and ask the Lord Jesus to abort every seed out of us that was not deposited in truth and in alignment with His perfect Will. However, every person has a choice. Either we choose to abort works of the flesh that are hindering our success or suffer the consequences of a spiritual miscarriage of Gods' promises. The Lord will not force any of us to make that choice. It is entirely up to you.

The Lord spoke to the children of Israel in the book of Exodus that they would come face to face with their enemy.

Exodus 23:20-24 (KJV) *[20] "Behold, I send an Angel before thee, to keep thee in the way, and to bring thee into the place which I have prepared." [21] "Beware of him, and obey his voice, provoke him not; for he will not pardon your transgressions: for my name is in him." [22] "But if thou shalt indeed obey his voice, and do all that I speak; then I will be an enemy unto thine enemies, and an adversary unto thine adversaries." [23] "For mine Angel shall go before thee, and bring thee in unto the Amorites, and the Hittites, and the Perizzites, and the Canaanites, the Hivites, and the Jebusites: and I will cut them off." [24] "Thou shalt not bow* *down to their gods, nor serve them, nor do after their works: but thou shalt utterly overthrow them, and quite break down their images."*

It is sometimes difficult to come face to face with the issues that have caused a person to fall short of their divine destiny. In reading this scripture, one might ask "Why would the Angel lead the children of Israel to their own enemy?" If a Believer is praying and seeking God, why wouldn't God just destroy the enemy instead. However, note that the Lord did promise to cut the enemy off in vs. 22, but only if they chose to obey. He would be an enemy to their enemy and an adversary to their adversary. The Amorites, the Hivites, the Hittites, the Perizzites, and the Canaanites were in possession of territory that belonged to the Children of Israel, but they had to come face to face with their enemy in order to walk into the land that God has promised them. We must consider this same message of application to our lives today. To get to our place of purpose and destiny, we must come face to face with issues we may be uncomfortable dealing with.

In these last days, there is going to be a release of Satanic power like we have never seen before. How many of us would have thought of the day we would have to be concerned about someone coming into the House of God and shooting innocent people. This level of demonic power need vessels to operate in. Because of this, there is an urgency for Believers to get out of the natural realm of flesh and arm ourselves with spiritual weapons of warfare. This cannot happen if One chooses not to deal with their personal issues and ask God to remove every seed from within that is hindering God's purpose for their life. We've heard preaching for many years on sins of the flesh, such as fornication, adultery, etc. with less focus on sins of the spirit. If Satan can keep an individual bound with iniquity in their heart, they will become a target vessel for the deposit of familiar spirits that will seduce those who are weak and carnal minded. Every part of man must be equipped in these last days.

1 Thessalonians 5:23 (KJV) *²³"And the very God of peace sanctify you wholly; and I pray God your whole spirit and soul and body be preserved blameless unto the coming of our Lord Jesus Christ."*

We must strive to make certain that every part of our lives (body, soul and spirit) is properly nourished to avoid a miscarriage of our purpose that positions us for success. However, again it is a choice. And because many have made bad choices, they tend to become bitter and indifferent with others for no reason, other than that they are unhappy with themselves. Your body is the temple of the Holy Spirit and should be kept healthy by eating the right diet and getting the proper amount of rest. Your mind and your spirit need to be renewed daily by the Word of God.

Romans 12:2-3 (KJV) *2 "And be not conformed to this world: but be ye transformed by the renewing of your mind, that ye may prove what is that good, and acceptable, and perfect, will of God." 3 "For I say, through the grace given unto me, to every man that is among you, not to think of himself more highly than he ought to think; but to think soberly, according as God hath dealt to every man the measure of faith."*

Fasting and Prayer helps to keep your spirit more open to hear the voice of God to receive instruction for your life. Always consider that if we do not take time to nourish the total man (body, soul, and spirit), Satan will take care of it for you and the works of the flesh will become the hindrance to fulfilling what you were called to do in the earth. There is no insurance that will cover the cost of disobedience to God. But there is an assurance and life insurance in obedience to His Will and His Word.

Take a moment and evaluate the things you need to willfully abort out of your heart that may have been there for some time. You may have to dig deep and be very honest. Maybe get in a quiet place, away from everyone and write down those things you know are causing you to see yourself as unsuccessful and worthless that may be hindering your success. Decide to let it all go!! Start today by releasing every false perception of who you are by allowing the Spirit of the Lord to heal the pain of the past. Get ready to speak into your own life what the enemy has said would never be. We will discover in the next two chapters how to do just that.

"There is Greatness in you."

50

CHAPTER 6

The End View Mirror

Life is a journey filled with challenges, opportunities, and oppositions. How we choose to deal with these factors will determine one's level of success. Additionally, how you see yourself will determine the level of respect as to how others see you. Every person may not like you, but your mission to succeed will command respect, regardless. God has a plan for our lives; you should have a plan for your own life, or others will create a plan for you.

Jeremiah 29:11 (KJV) *[11]"For I know the thoughts that I think toward you, saith the LORD, thoughts of peace, and not of evil, to give you an expected end."*

Gods' plan is to give us an expected end that is not based on a reminder of times when we have failed or missed Him. They are thoughts of peace and not of evil. However, this is not the plan that the enemy has envisioned. He comes to steal, kill and destroy. And if we don't take full control of our lives and plan well, leaving behind past failures and past hurts, these things will become the driving force for your future. Planning starts with setting goals. Goals that are realistic and can be achieved in small increments until the full plan is executed. Many people fail because they try to do too much at one time. This is sometimes due to the need to try and impress others. Just be you! As mentioned in earlier chapters, success is defined within the walls of your assignment, not within the walls of another man's accomplishments.

If you are too tired to do what you have been called to do, you are probably doing something you were not called to do, and it is taking all of your energy.

Stop It Today!! ...before you burnout

You should never set goals that are strictly related to the norm. The most successful people were creative beyond traditional thinking. They took a risk and had confidence within themselves to trust their gut. Have you ever said to yourself, "I sense something in my gut?"

Many of us have had the sense that something was just not right in many situations, or something in your gut gave you a sense that you were making the right decision. However, there is a spiritual revelation to this fact. We were all made in the image and likeness of God. Every part of our bodies has a purpose, and the gut is sometimes considered our second brain. It is that subconscious part of the nervous system that links to the many nerves in the belly that gives us a gut feeling regarding certain matters. Paul said it like this ......Let this mind be in you, as also was in Christ Jesus **(Phil. 2:5)**. To think like Christ requires a willingness to seek to know His voice when He speaks.

John 10:27-28 (KJV) *27 "My sheep hear my voice, and I know them, and they follow me."*

Knowing and hearing God's voice will never be a reality if you choose to think on a level that does not challenge the status quo. Jesus was so wise that His responses raised the attention of the well learned. He knew how to address every level of thought by responding in such a way that took them where they had never been. Can you take your thoughts and level of creativity to a place where others have never been by allowing the Mind of Christ to direct your thinking? Consider what happened at the tower of Babel. They were so creative with the wrong motive that God had to come down and stop the plan.

Your End View should never be through the lens of the Now, but a projection into the future of what God has predestined for you to achieve.

You start by getting rid of the box that man has created and start writing your own storyline. Paul reminds us that we are living Epistles.

2 Corinthians 3:2 (KJV) *² "Ye are our epistle written in our hearts, known and read of all men."*

Thinking outside the box is traditional, getting rid of the box all together, and then start thinking is Kingdom

This is challenging for many, because you take the risk of being viewed as someone who rocks the boat. And for those who are spiritual, you are viewed as someone who is not hearing from God, because it does not align with what most are accustomed to. We are living more comfortable lives because somebody went from thinking mail by mailbox delivery to email by technology; from website to social media; from the extreme expenses of television ministry to Face Book live free. But you must be willing to let go of perceiving that man's way is always God's way.

Isaiah 55:8-9 (KJV) *⁸ "For my thoughts are not your thoughts, neither are your ways my ways, saith the LORD." ⁹ "For as the heavens are higher than the* *earth, so are my ways higher than your ways, and my thoughts than your thoughts."*

Envision what you see through your *End View Mirror* that may challenge you to get rid of the box all together. If that view is in alignment with the plan of God for your life, His Word, and expanding the Kingdom with God ordained principles.... the sky is the limit.   Where do you see yourself five to ten years from today? Hopefully, it is not in the same place you are now if you believe in living a progressive life. You must set realistic goals that align with God's perfect Will for your life and not be detracted. The ability to stay focused during opposition speaks to one's level of maturity. Take hold of your destiny and don't give up.

Hebrews 11:1 (KJV) *[11] "Now faith is the substance of things hoped for, the evidence of things not seen."*

As we close this chapter, let's reference again, the mindset of the people at the tower of babel in the book of Genesis the Eleventh Chapter. They all spoke the same language, their motives were unified, and they saw themselves achieving their goal in the end. Their ambition to succeed was so powerful that it got the attention of the Lord. If He had not come down to confound the languages, the people would have achieved their goal with the wrong motive.

Genesis 11 (KJV) *¹ "And the whole earth was of one language, and of one speech. ² And it came to pass, as they journeyed from the east, that they found a plain in the land of Shinar; and they dwelt there. ³ And they said one to another, Go to, let us make brick, and burn them thoroughly. And they had brick for stone, and slime had they for morter. ⁴ And they said, Go to, let us build us a city and a tower, whose top may reach unto heaven; and let us make us a name, lest we be scattered abroad upon the face of the whole earth. ⁵ And the Lord came down to see the city and the tower, which the children of men builded. ⁶ And the Lord said, Behold, the people is one, and they have all one language; and this they begin to do: and now nothing will be restrained from them, which they have imagined to do. ⁷ Go to, let us go down, and there confound their language, that they may not understand one another's speech. ⁸ So the Lord scattered them abroad from thence upon the face of all the earth: and they left off to build the city."*

There are lessons to be learned from this biblical text that each of us should apply to our daily lives. To sum it all up, nothing can constrain you from achieving your goals, but you and how you see yourself at the conclusion of the matter. If you see yourself as being successful, and you apply the right principles of hard work, being persistent, never wavering, with faith in God through every opposition... you will succeed.

Joshua 1:8 (KJV) *⁸ "This book of the law shall not depart out of thy mouth; but thou shalt meditate therein day and night, that thou mayest observe to do according to all that is written therein: for then thou shalt make thy way prosperous, and then thou shalt have good success."*

In the next final chapter, we will conclude this matter with how important it is to speak the Word into your own life.

What you see is not always what you get, but it is what you speak. **Proverbs 18:21 (KJV)** *²¹Death and life are in the power of the tongue: and they that love it shall eat the fruit thereof.*

58

CHAPTER 7

The Miracle of Mirror Talk

Let's further examine the profound words of wisdom in **Proverbs 18:21** that concludes with the outcome related to what we speak. Notice the scripture says... *and they that love it shall eat the fruit thereof.* Love what? Whatever comes out of your mouth. So, if you love to speak positive things into your life, positive things will eventually come to you. If you love having a pity party by speaking negative things into your life, then negative things will come to you. Whether it be good fruit or bad fruit, your words will determine which it will be.

It appears that this proverb is trying to help us to understand that our emotions play a significant part in what we say.

Luke 6:45 (KJV) *45 "A good man out of the good treasure of his heart bringeth forth that which is good; and an evil man out of the evil treasure of his heart bringeth forth that which is evil: for of the abundance of the heart his mouth speaketh."*

It is our emotions (soul) that determine how we respond or react to any given situation. This is the reason why one should never allow anyone to possess their soul (i.e. emotions, thoughts). People who have the need to manipulate others' thinking to gratify their own self-worth, have not discovered who they really are. They live to live out their success by devaluing the worth of others. You must be wise enough to discern this in others around you, so it does not distract you from moving forward with your goals in life. As discussed earlier, do not own issues that have nothing to do with you.

Because what we experience in life does impact our emotions, it in turn will impact what we say. Out of the abundance of the heart, does a man speak. So, the emphasis here should be to protect your heart, your spirit. Jesus had three disciples that were really close to him...Peter, James and John. Although Jesus picked the other disciples, He clearly had a different level of relationship with each of them. Consider Judas, whom Jesus picked as one of His disciples. He knew that Judas would portray him, and Peter would deny him.

Matthew 26:24-26 (KJV) *24 "The Son of man goeth as it is written of him: but woe unto that man by whom the Son of man is betrayed! it had been good for that man if he had not been born. 25 Then Judas, which betrayed him, answered and said, Master, is it*

I? He said unto him, Thou hast said. ²⁶And as they were eating, Jesus took bread, and blessed it, and brake it, and gave it to the disciples, and said, Take, eat; this is my body."

Take note how Jesus dealt with what he knew, by his response to Judas... *"Thou hast said."* Jesus' response validated that people know what they are doing, and sadly sometimes they think others do not, but their words reveal what is in their heart. Notice in the twenty-sixth verse that Jesus did not allow what He knew about Judas, of whom He chose as one of His disciples, to distract him from His purpose. Jesus kept it moving, without delay. We must learn to do the same when God has revealed to us exactly what we are dealing with. As mentioned earlier, you must do your research about your geographical area, pay attention to things around you (i.e. watch and pray), choose relationships carefully (but don't be afraid to trust again) and finally be a good listener.

Being a good listener is a characteristic that one must have to stay ahead of the enemy. Everything that is said to you does not require an immediate response, or not even a response at all.

1 Thessalonians 4:11 (KJV) *[11]"And that ye study to be quiet, and to do your own business, and to work with your own hands, as we commanded you."*

Your life is a window for some and a mirror for others. There are those who will watch your life, see you as a role model, and aspire to mirror your success. There are others who are just watching through the window trying to see what they can hold against you. You can defeat this paradigm by not allowing how others see you to be the final chapter of your life. Set your own goals and see yourself achieving them. Begin to speak into your own future what you desire in life and what you know God has promised.

My husband started a car detailing business after we moved from Florida to the Atlanta area. Although he had retired, along with being a disabled veteran, he did not stop dreaming. He was persistent when others disagreed. I would always say... "Why are you working like this?" "You need to rest." However, he kept it moving with vision. After a few years in business, his work van broke down and he needed another vehicle. The cost to repair the van was not worth the investment. By faith he kept saying... "Somebody is going to give me a truck." And he kept saying it repeatedly. Until one day, one of his customers gave him a 2008 Nissan double cab truck, paid in full that looked brand new. A few months later, my son-in-law's truck broke down, and he desperately needed another truck for his construction business. This same customer, said to my husband one day... "John looks like you need another truck, this cab is a little small for your equipment." Of course, my husband responded with a positive "yes", with a smile on his face. The customer gave my husband another truck that he chose to give to my son-in law, who needed another truck for his business.

The lesson to be learned here is to keep speaking what seems impossible. My husband kept saying what he believed until it came to pass. Not only did it come to pass for him, but for someone else who was also in need.

The gift of giving is the fertilizer for multiplication. Don't be selfish

My husband could have easily said, I will keep this truck for myself. However, God knew his heart was to give, and he could be trusted with extra. Can you be trusted with extra, after you have spoken things into your life and God granted you more than enough? This is another key to success. If you give sparingly, you will reap sparingly. If you give bountifully, you will reap bountifully (**II Corinth. 9:6**).

The journey to success to reach your divine destiny begins with your words. Stand in the mirror and talk to yourself. Speak life and not death. Declare what the enemy has said would never be... as already done. Whether others believe you or not, can you speak the Word when others disagree? Many times, we throw away our blessings because during times of hardship, we accept the verdict of defeat that has been handed down by public opinion. Learn to be a risk taker with more than one plan.

Consider Nehemiah when they set out to rebuild the walls of Jerusalem. There was so much rubbish that it looked like an impossible task. And there were those who came to help but did not have Nehemiah's vision at heart.

Ezra 4 King (KJV) *[1] "Now when the adversaries of Judah and Benjamin heard that the children of the captivity builded the temple unto the LORD God of Israel; [2] Then they came to Zerubbabel, and to the chief of the fathers, and said unto them, Let us build with you: for we seek your God, as ye do; and we do* *sacrifice unto him since the days of Esarhaddon king of Assur, which brought us up hither. ³But Zerubbabel, and Jeshua, and the rest of the chief of the fathers of Israel, said unto them, Ye have nothing to do with us to build an house unto our God; but we ourselves together will build unto the LORD God of Israel, as king Cyrus the king of Persia hath commanded us. ⁴Then the people of the land weakened the hands of the people of Judah, and troubled them in building, ⁵And hired counsellors against them, to frustrate their purpose, all the days of Cyrus king of Persia, even until the reign of Darius king of Persia."*

There will be those who cross your path who will not have your vision or best interest at heart. But don't be distracted. Always have a Plan B and sometimes a Plan C and D. In other words, plan to never be defeated. Nehemiah had a plan behind the walls, in strategic places. He was determined to rebuild the walls of Jerusalem.

While the enemy is plotting, you should be planning

Nehemiah 4:17 (KJV) *¹"But it came to pass, that when Sanballat heard that we builded the wall, he was wroth, and took great indignation, and* *mocked the Jews. ²And he spake before his brethren and the army of Samaria, and said, What do these feeble Jews? will they fortify themselves? will they sacrifice? will they make an end in a day? will they revive the stones out of the heaps of the rubbish which are burned? ³Now Tobiah the Ammonite was by him, and he said, Even that which they build, if a fox go up, he shall even break down their stone wall. ⁴Hear, O our God; for we are despised: and turn their reproach upon their own head, and give them for a prey in the land of captivity: ⁵And cover not their iniquity, and let not their sin be blotted out from before thee: for they have provoked thee to anger before the builders. ⁶So built we the wall; and all the wall was joined together unto the half thereof: for the people had a mind to work. ⁷But it came to pass, that when Sanballat, and Tobiah, and the Arabians, and the Ammonites, and the Ashdodites, heard that the walls of Jerusalem were made up, and that the breaches began to be stopped, then they were very wroth, ⁸And conspired all of them together to come and to fight against Jerusalem, and to hinder it. ⁹Nevertheless we made our prayer unto our God, and set a watch against them day and night, because of them. ¹⁰And Judah said, The strength of the bearers of burdens is decayed, and there is much rubbish; so that we are not able to build the wall. [11] And our adversaries said, They shall not know, neither see, till we come in the midst among them, and slay them, and cause the work to cease. [12] And it came to pass, that when the Jews which dwelt by them came, they said unto us ten times, From all places whence ye shall return unto us they will be upon you. [13] Therefore set I in the lower places behind the wall, and on the higher places, I even set the people after their families with their swords, their spears, and their bows."*

So, let's recap the seven principles outlined in each chapter of this book that will help you in dismissing every altered reflection of yourself, and put you on the path to fulfilling your purpose and enjoy doing it!!

I.   Determine if how you see yourself is fact or is it a fictitious story line that you have accepted as fact.

II.   Learn the difference between internal and external issues that can cause unnecessary warfare when you internalize issues that have nothing to do with you.

III.   Avoid being intimate with your own issues but face it and overcome them.

IV.   Don't conceive spirits that will cause you to fight against your own purpose.

V. Let go of every negative seed that has been planted in your life that will cause you to lose what God has predestined for your success.

VI. See yourself winning in the End.

VII. Begin to speak victory into your own life and choose to never be defeated.

Bishop John Crenshaw's prayer manual *"I Agree"* How to Pray the Word When Others Disagree, will show you how to develop a prayer life that will help you to stay focused on speaking the Word of God into every situation of your life, in spite of the opposition. Start today setting strategic goals, pray for direction and stay focused despite public opinion. It is your time to live and enjoy all the riches of God's blessings for your life.

Greater is He that is in You than He that is in the World!!

In the End you Win!!

Say it right now... "In the end I win!"

Believe it and confess it daily and watch God!

CHAPTER 8

New Beginnings

This is your chapter to begin writing your own story that is fact and not fiction. Set your goals, ask God for a strategic plan, do your research and execute without delay. Don't be distracted by the naysayers and the status quo. Be unique in your assignment as the Lord has given it to you. Remember these quotes as you begin to write your story. One day your story will be a written epistle for others to be blessed and inspired.

Thinking outside the box is traditional, but getting rid of the box all together, and then start thinking is Kingdom.

While the enemy is plotting, you should be planning.

What you see is not always what you get, but it is what you speak.

If this book has ignited another level of passion to succeed and accomplish your life's dreams, then start writing your vision now and don't delay. Space has been provided for those who are serious about their next level to begin the journey of living your best life and enjoy all the riches of God's divine favor.

Let's go!!

Identify and list the altered reflections that have hindered your success.

____

____

____

____

____

____

____

____

____

____

____

____

____

Set realistic goals (i.e. where do you see yourself in the next 5-10 years)

____

____

____

____

____

____

____

____

____

____

____

____

____

____

____

____

____

____

Now, let's begin to write your own story and see yourself accomplishing your goals. (Remember to include the Lord as an integral part of your story)

____

____

____

____

____

____

____

____

____

____

____

____

____

____

____

____

____

____

About

Dr. Janice Crenshaw

Dr. Janice Crenshaw is a passionate innovative organizational leader and Minister of the Gospel with decades of experience in healthcare and ministry. She has traveled across the United States, London, West Africa, South Africa, and Germany, spreading the Good News of Jesus Christ, as a conference speaker and gospel singer.

She is the President of Excel Community Development Corp. a 501c3 organization that has the mission of equipping individuals with biblically based tools to change their own world. The lives of hundreds of women, including those who were previously incarcerated, have been transformed thru the Excel empowerment curriculum and are now living productive, successful lives after their release.

Dr. Janice Crenshaw is passionate about giving back to the community to inspire change and growth in every aspect of one's life, to include a global mission that partners with other non-profit organizations and businesses, locally and abroad in support of food relief, empowerment programs for families, and resourcing materials and empowerment tools to Africa to help change the trajectory of individual's lives.

She blends her expertise in healthcare, leadership, and ministry to deliver compelling, life-changing messages. Her God given wisdom and knowledge, combined with her dynamic and relatable speaking style, empowers individuals, organizations, and congregations to rise to their fullest potential. She is the author of seven books and three gospel recording CDs.

Consider this may be your next book!

To order more books and product by Dr. Janice Crenshaw

Go to www.drjanicecrenshaw.com